In my own words

Written by Lillybelle

Illustrated by Jenna Goddard

I dedicate this book to everyone in my perfectly imperfect family –
you have all helped me to become me.

A special thanks to my mama for sharing her love of writing with me
and giving me a way to share my feelings.

To Jenna and Jade for bringing my story to life!

I love you all.

Hello, I'm Lillybelle. I am 6 years old.

I love reading,

dancing,

singing,

and beautiful flowers. Well, I am named after a flower after all!

I am clever, kind and a little bit cheeky.

I always try my best to be helpful
even though sometimes
people think I am annoying.

I am Lillybelle.

I am all these things.
I am also adopted.

Being adopted means living with a new family who will
love you as their own.

Before I was adopted, I lived with a foster carer. A foster carer is someone who takes care of you if your birth family can't, while decisions are made about the best place for you to be.

My foster carers name was Jayne.

Jayne and her family were Awesome!

They took great care of me and my little brother. So, I felt sad at first when I was told that we were going to be adopted.

Jayne said that we could keep in touch with her and that made me feel a bit better.

When my adoptive mummy and daddy came to meet me for the first time, I felt nervous, but pleased that me and my brother got to stay together.

I worried that they might not like me, or that I might not like them.

They were strangers to me.

Everyone always says, "Don't talk to strangers"

Now I have to live with them?

Hello again, it's been a while. 5 years to be precise.

I'm 11 now.

I love dogs, cats, horses, animals in general really.

I love my friends, my school, drawing, painting, writing, but most of all I love my family. You know, those strangers I met 5 years ago!

We have a lot to catch up on don't we. So, let's go back to when we last spoke. I was 6, my foster carer Jayne had told me that I had a new family that I was going to live with, and I was feeling nervous.

If I could go back and talk to my 6-year-old self I would tell myself this,

life gets good!

It didn't always feel so good though.

Not when I was 3 and had to leave my birth family.

Not when I was 6 and had to leave my foster family.

It was a long drive from my foster family to my mummy and daddy's house.

I don't remember much about the drive now, but I do remember arriving at my new home and thinking WOW, it was beautiful.

For a little while I felt like I was in a dream.

My mummy and daddy were nice. We did lots of fun things together. Mummy gave me cool hair styles with lots of pretty bows.

Daddy baked cakes with me and twirled me around in the living room to Disney music.

We were always outside walking our dog who I love. He gives the best cuddles and reminds me of the dog I had when I was little with my birth family.

I miss her.

Mummy and daddy tell me they love me every single day and I believe them.

They tell me that out of all the children in the whole world needing a new family, me and my brothers are the most perfect for them.

I love my family.

But I also miss my birth family.

When I was 6, I would cry for them. Now I'm 11 I mostly just wonder about them.
I wonder what they are doing, if they are alright and if they miss me.

Mummy says that I am unforgettable.

In the moments that I feel sad, mummy holds me and listens to my memories.

I always feel better after a cry and a cuddle.

This year I am starting secondary school. It feels big and scary just like being adopted did.

Except this time, I know that I can do big and scary things.

I have awesome (although slightly annoying) little brothers.
I have a mummy and daddy who make me feel safe and loved.
I have a happy home and a happy heart.

I don't know where my life will take me, but I do know this, I am going to make it good...

No,

AMAZING!

Because I am amazing and deserving of amazing things. If you're reading this, then **so are you!**

Yeah, life gets good!

Printed in Great Britain
by Amazon